Pouring My Love In Broken Vessels

The Relationship Reference Guide

Kimberly W. Massey

ISBN: **10-0989844900**

ISBN 13: **978-0-9898449-0-1**

Gebrae Publishing Group: **Tampa, Florida**

Dedication

*To my children – Gene and Abrae', you are my
life support.
To my daddy – Bobby Gleaton, you are the
foundation that anchors me.*

.

CONTENTS

FOREWORD

For so long, I have prayed that God would send a clear and concise word to help our women succeed in identifying their potential mate. Church women, corporate women, and women of all ethnicities, cultures, ages, and class systems needed a tool for discernment apart from emotional and sexual attachments. They needed factual data that is Biblically sound so that when decisions are being made concerning their mate, they are being made using the intellect of the Spirit and not the frailties of our flesh. As a Pastor, I daily counsel those who "fail in love" instead of "falling in love," so it has always been my desire to find a handbook to assist our sisters in Christ. They needed a manual, a tour guide if you will, to help them critically assess and analyze their potential mate before they even consider committing themselves in the covenant relationship of marriage.

Fortunately for us, God has answered my prayers and has written through the pen of Pastor Kimberly Massey. Pouring My Love In Broken Vessels The Relationship Reference Guide is rightful access to the insight of heaven itself. Pastor Massey has created relatable characters; characters that compel all of us to reflect on our own past relationships. This book is a masterful way of pulling together all those Biblical nuggets we learned throughout our church experiences and placing them into a narrative that is easily read and easily received. If you are ready to take the limitations off of your life, I suggest you keep reading. You can enjoy this read because it will empower and equip you, ensuring that you are never again the victim of another broken vessel.

Pastor Ronald Godbee
The River Church
Durham, North Carolina

CHAPTER 1

I Am a Gallon;
He Is a Shot Glass

*The simplicity of just being me has often
proven to be too much for many of the
male suitors who I have engaged.*

There is something so very special about
the first date. Although it is exhilarat-
ing, it is equally debilitating. It brings with
it a mixed of hopeful possibilities and the
anticipation of yet another rejection. As

women, we go through the painstaking rituals of presenting our best. After all, everyone knows that first impressions are often lasting ones. We also take into account that we feel the competition of every female who has endeared herself to him in the past. On top of that, at dinner the overly friendly, nicely shaped hostess switches her five-times-a-week-at-the-gym derriere to guide us to our table.

We fiercely battle the images that are craftily airbrushed across magazines; they do not accurately depict the beauty of a real woman with real curves and "acceptable flaws." Our credit card debts are reflections of our increasing desire to have the fashion savvy of the current starlet, with our savings accounts bearing the burden of sheer nothingness. We quickly race to our hairstylist, nail technician, favorite boutique, and for some, local lingerie store just to get the goggle-eyed compliment of this potential love interest. All of this only to find out that he has already determined in his mind he is not spending any more on this date than what is necessary to get a sip of our "happy juice."

I would give you spiced wine to drink,
the juice of my pomegranates.
Song of Solomon 8:2

The expenditures that both parties invested in the first date are typically the barometer for the remainder of the relationship. Why? Because what happens then can show that, although I am a gallon, he is a shot glass. I have the capacity to love a whole lot more than he does! That is my personality, my genetic make-up. I want to put my best foot forward at all times. I want to exemplify the spirit of excellence. "Wholeness" is my middle name, and perfection is my game. I bring it big, or I stay at home. I laugh big, and I live even bigger. I awaken thinking of creative ways to make him happy. I smile when I feel I have originated a romantic idea that is multi-layered in execution. I am consumed by the idea that there is one, only one, who will and can anticipate my arrival on the scene of his existence.

The ideal man who is my prince is surely praying for me. He has diligently sought the Lord and yielded himself, just as I have, to a life of purity and self-control. The Bible says, "He who finds a wife, finds a good thing and obtains favor of the Lord" (Proverbs 18:22). Oh yes, Baby, he is at the altar right now learning how to love me just like I love him. He will recognize when I am discouraged. He will completely support my dreams and endeavors. He will use his strong hands to caress me and not ever use them as a weapon against me. His words will be music that beats to the rhythm of God's Word. He is the gentleman who opens car doors and doors of opportunity. This man is my partner, protector, and BFF for life. He is the vessel who is a gallon like me.

So why have most of my relationships been with "shot-glass-capacity" men? They have been the very opposite of who I am and what I am supposed to have! My very existence overwhelms them. The casting of my vision invokes waves of insecurity in the puddles of their sightlessness. They muster enough courage to approach me, with the same chanting of the children's rhyme, "I think I can, I think I can, I think I can." They see the gallon. They want the gallon. They can receive from the gallon, but they can contribute only what they are to the gallon: a shot glass full.

The Law of Reciprocity means that giving and taking, cause and effect, are mutually exchanged. In other words, you reap only what you have sown. Again, this lends itself to the idea of capacity and the ability to give and receive. Jesus gives us much insight about this concept in Luke 12:48: *From everyone who has been given much, much will be demanded. And from the one trusted with much, much more will be expected.* Although all men are created equal, all men do not have the capacity to love equally.

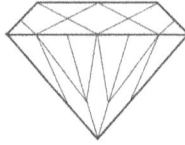

Pink Diamond

**People cannot give you more
than they have themselves.**

Capacity is a simple concept. It is the
power to receive or contain. It is twofold in
nature, both working toward one objective.
Let's take for example a kitchen strainer
basket: it has the ability to receive. However, its primary purpose is not to hold all
that it receives but to support the solid that
is too thick to be filtered through. In that
same kitchen, the strainer is often used
within the sink. The sink has the same purpose as a strainer only in a greater dimen-
sion and with some functionary exceptions.
The sink has a larger capacity, but it is de-
signed to allow a pour-through as well. In
close proximity, there are multiple cabinets
that store all styles and sizes of containers,
with lids, that will contain what they re-

ceive. They all receive but have different options for containing what is received.

The idea of capacity in everyday life is easily understood and often is determined by the use of common sense. You look for a vessel large enough to contain what must be poured into it. If it doesn't fit, you don't force it. Although the same principle applies, love and relationships are not so easily calculated. The walls of the heart cannot be measured by the metric system. The depth of the emotions can't be ascertained by just a glance. The capacity to receive and contain love often is not realized until time has been invested. You have actually begun the process of showering parts of your love and life onto this guy before you realize that something is not flowing quite as smoothly as you would like. Although you give because it is just who you are, you are noticing that there is a void inside your soul.

The hallmark of a gallon/shot glass relationship is that the gallon person never experiences the benefit of being in a relationship with the shot glass. The shot-glass man is stressed, frustrated, and often angry because he will not and can never fulfill the needs of a gallon woman. Even when he gives all that he has the capacity to give, it is only a drop in the proverbial bucket.

The root of this problem stems from the innate characteristic of being a nurturer. God created a woman to be a nurturer by nature. The anatomical proof is the presence of a womb in the body of a woman. It is the only organ created to nurture the life and existence of another person. This ability to nurture reaches far beyond our physical structure to influence how we nurture the people and the things in relation to us.

Sadly, when we meet this man who has a limited capacity to give love and receive love, we shift into "nurturing gear" and overcompensate in giving our love to "grow" the relationship. In essence, the gift that we are supposed to give to our children and to our dreams we mistakenly extend to emotionally underdeveloped men. Ladies, this sentiment is misplaced! You are

POURING MY LOVE IN BROKEN VESSELS

to love the man and nurture the relationship. Just as an embryo is the creation of both male and female contributions and is nourished deep within the core of a woman's body, a relationship should be the product of both the man and the woman's contributions. *Then* you can nurture what is formed from that union. You cannot supply everything in the relationship and expect it to be happy and sustainable.

THE SIGNS AND SYMPTOMS

Spiritually:

You initiate all of your Godly encounters as a couple.

You are the one who suggests and leads the majority of prayers. You are constantly encouraging him to attend church.

You are the only one taking a stand in the relationship toward purity in your lifestyle.

11

He is consistently urging you to abandon your faithfulness to God for him.

He minimizes and devalues your Godliness and Christian conduct. He often makes excuses for his lack of motivation concerning Godliness.

Emotionally:

You are vocal regarding your feelings for him. You say, "I love you" and he responds, "I care about you."

You are openly sharing your commitment to him with others. He does not give you access to his world.

You have forgiven him multiple times for the same offense. He shows no signs of changing his mind or his behavior.

CHAPTER 2

The Shattered-Glass Man

Michelle is the quintessential modern woman every other woman wants to be and every man wants. She is also a committed Christian. Always finding outlets of improvement and self-discovery, Michelle is well-rounded and sociable. Although she doesn't possess the plastic-surgery-perfected image of Hollywood, she has learned to accept and accentuate her beauty strengths and work them well.

Michelle is experiencing the happiest moments of her entire life because she is finally planning the wedding of her dreams. With the fierce confidence that is characteristic of her personality, she sashays into the bridal boutique to add the most important item to her registry. So far she has made sure to coordinate every single detail to perfection: "Ecru, not beige, and it is mauve not lavender!"

"Michelle, let's choose your china collection today. Would you like traditional or modern?" the sales clerks asks with delight. "Well, Arlene, you know I want something classy, distinctive, and, of course, functional. Do you have something with a French Provincial Renaissance influence?" Clapping with happiness and relief that this bride knows specifically what she wants and absolutely knows what she will not have, Arlene quickly moves to the rear of the brightly lit showcase. "I have the exact collection that you are looking for; I am sure that you will highly approve of these pieces!"

Arlene carefully reaches for the most expensively priced place setting in the market. Michelle's bubbly attitude promptly becomes contemplative as she meticulously examines every inch of each container. She is precise, analytical, and very careful to search for any possible flaws. She calculates the functionality of these pieces into her vision of beauty and decorum. All of this with painstaking energy, observation, time, and prayer…yes, prayer. With a sigh of relief and fulfillment, she finally decides that this style is the right choice of china for her lifestyle. Too bad Michelle did not use these principles to decide her most important decision about her wedding plans: her groom! Unlike the china collection she has so prudently chosen, her husband-to-be is a shattered vessel.

"It is easier to build strong children than to repair broken men," advised Frederick Douglas about when to lay the tenets of a whole, intact character inside of a man. The most impactful, effective, and long-lasting way to shape men is when the bitterness of bias does not course through the veins of their souls. Instead, character is best molded when they are boys whose hearts are yet tender and whose minds have not been tainted with the venom of betrayal and the poison of hatred. Unfortunately, the gross reality we are forced to accept is that our world is filled with broken men. Many of them have been mishandled, abused, and left without a healing balm or being directed to a cure. As with the evolution of any disease or disparity, this condition may go undetected by the natural eye. Although unseen, it is no less destructive. The sphere of love and romance are no different.

You think you can easily identify a *shattered-glass man*. His tiny pieces of glass are spread about, hopeless of ever being restored to its originally intended form. However, you might think that he has been shattered by an *explosion*.Grab your cognitive remote control and change the channel of your thoughts. An explosion happens because energy is transmitted outwardly. Consequently, the debris of that force blows out and is spread abroad. In contrast, the shattered-glass man, who has multiple issues, has been broken by *implosion* — a sudden collapse. It is an internal destruction that has better control over when and where the debris lands. This guy is well put together and intact on the outside, but there are multiple shards in his psyche-mindset and values. The right set of circumstances and the wrong woman will cause this man to suddenly fall to pieces.

Chancellor is a cool, tall glass of chocolate milk. He is what previous generations would call, "the cat's meow" or "the bee's knees." Although his visit to the gym four times a week is evident in his rock-hard body and six-pack abs, he really is down-to-earth and easy to approach. He enjoys the benefits that his sales route job provides by constantly putting him in contact with a variety of attractive women, many of whose telephone numbers are on his speed dial. Minister Chancellor has led the single men's group at church for the last three years. During the monthly meetings of fellowship, he constantly encourages the guys that he mentors not to be "womanizers" who sleep with multiple women. "Remember that Jesus' mother was a woman and your mother is a woman!" They nod with familiar reception and repeat his mantra with him. Having been raised by an independent, highly educated, entrepreneurial, single mother, Chancellor champions the cause of women's rights.

The question that seems to always work itself into conversation with Chancellor among his acquaintances, family, and church members is: "Why isn't a guy like you married?" He quickly dispels any idea of being bi-sexual or gay, which he certainly is not. When questioning him, they bring up the beautiful model who accompanied him to the annual church BBQ two years ago, or they *hint* about the investment banker who is rapidly rising to the ranks of a local real estate mogul. His buddies "high five" him about the choir member who is built like a brick house, suggesting with grunts and grins that she would be the lady-in-the-street but freak-in-the-sheets type. The list of "could be, would be, and should be" goes on and on.

The trail of past relationships and scorned women is long enough to wrap around Chancellor's community — twice. Surely there has to be a woman who is suitable for this "catch." Many have tried the time-honored "getting to his heart through his stomach," and others have targeted their goals about four inches lower. When they finally reached his heart, they found a shame-faced, little third-grade boy who was labeled, "Delayed." Other women tried to perform acrobatic sexual exploits on him. He accepted the favors by reasoning that he is a man before he is a man of God. Yet these women learned that he did not value them beyond the momentary physical pleasure he received from them because he felt deep down inside that all women must hate all men. At least that is what his mother instilled in him by her critical words and cruel behaviors toward the men who were briskly in and out of her life.

Chancellor is great on the basketball court with his "boys," but often he runs into conflict with his managers and teachers and even has bouts with Reverend Preachwright. He doesn't have the initiative to start a business on his own, but he is resistant to guidance from potentially great male mentors. This behavior is a direct result of the Saturdays he spent waiting endless hours on the stoop with a baseball in one hand and a pint-sized mitt in the other for the father who was repeatedly a no-show. His dad demonstrated to Chancellor, by his lack of participation and commitment in his life, that everything and everyone was more important than Chancellor and his Little League game.

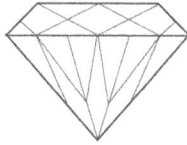

Pink Diamond

If he defies the authority figures in his life, he will never respect you.

Chancellor is eye candy with all of its trappings, but he is also a *shattered-glass man* with multiple issues. Everyone has issues, but a few indicators tell the difference between a good catch and a bad one. First is his willingness to acknowledge that there is an issue. After all, you cannot fix what you do not first acknowledge exists. Second is his willingness to accept the proper guidance and correction from positive resources. Finally is the presence of measureable, progressive change toward improvement. This is not an a la carte list. All three markers should exist before your stamp of approval.

CHAPTER 3

The Gaping-Hole Man—
What Goes In Comes Right
Back Out

Extreme loneliness can often influence our ability to make obvious and clearly correct choices. It is during these times that we most often enter and remain in relationships with people who obviously do not have the ability to be courtship material, let alone marriage ready. Although loneliness is the stated reason, low self-esteem ranks as the prevalent cause of "common-sense blindness." You come to a place where you are accepting of what *gaping-hole* guy presents, even though you are fully aware that it is subpar. Inwardly, you continue in this waste of a portion of your life and opportunities for other relationships because you feel that you may not get something better. You have resigned yourself to settle for maybe a minuscule hint of physical attraction, spiritual inclination, intellect, education, socio-economic condition, or even his interest in you.

The *gaping-hole* man has no ability to retain any of the goodness that pours from you. He simply can't! It really is not worth discussing all of the reasons why he cannot; the bottom line is the same result: whatever goes in comes directly out. The only positive thing about this type of relationship is that it reveals its terminal nature quickly. Assuming that you are whole and complete yourself, you can and will recognize the signs early in the process. Honestly, out of all the broken-vessel syndromes, this one was always the easiest to quickly dismiss, in my experience.

Holidays are especially difficult to manage when you are alone. This is "hog heaven" season for the *gaping-hole* man. Just as the holiday tables are spread with delicious high-calorie and fat-rich comfort foods, he finds comfort in the arms of many women. These women have a high potential for great relationships, but they have not yet been found by an honorable vessel. In order not to have the embarrassment of going to the company Christmas party alone, or bringing in the New Year unattached, they accept the guy who is 100 percent giving nothing but taking everything. He is the date who accompanies you to those numerous weddings. The entire time you are sporting a plastic smile and feigning happiness, your very essence is being drained dry.

The Grand Canyon, located in Arizona, has about five million visitors a year. Much of the fascination of this natural wonder is the vastness of its opening: 277 miles long,

18 miles wide, and 1 mile deep. The magnitude of this hole allows for several kinds of tours: airplane, hiking, rafting, and so forth. This American beauty also boasts of formations known as "uplift strata." The rich colors and geological diversity are captivating. The grandeur presented in this massive hole captures an average look of only about seventeen minutes though. After all, how much can be gleaned from looking into a gaping hole?

Sharlese's monthly dinner gathering with the girls reinforced what she already knew but certainly did not want to be reminded of every single time they convened. Like the precision of a finely tuned grandfather clock, appetizers would be shared with detailed debriefings of everyone's independent career advancements, or lack thereof. The main course would follow, served alongside a hefty dish of homemade, sisterhood advice.

"Sharlese, girl, are you still seeing...umm...?" Tina snapped her perfectly manicured fingers in rapid succession.

POURING MY LOVE IN BROKEN VESSELS

"What's his face?" It was indeed a rhetorical question. Tina already knew "the scoop" because Liv had filled her in after accidentally running into Sharlese and Arrington during brunch last week at a local hot spot. "Well." Sharlese offered a deliberate pause, hoping and praying for an interruption from the focus of attention she had become. She thought it would be a great time for the waiter to offer dessert. What happened to that baby who cried fifteen minutes nonstop when they first arrived? She hesitantly filled in the silence with her longstanding justification statement: "It's complicated."

The faithfully anticipated sighs, lip-popping grins, glasses toasting, and salsa music always accompanied the tongue-lashing that she received from her peers. *"Really?"* Melody gawked. The most outspoken of the group, her twice-divorced, in-between-relationships perspective was less than hopeful at its best. Sydney, the oldest of the group, began her "mother knows best" approach by saying, "Baby, we just want the best for you." Tavie, the licensed counseling clinician and most sophisticated of the bunch, with the ease of treating one of her emotionally derailed patients, chimed in: "You really need to seek professional help as to why you continue to attract the same type of man in every relationship you have had." Reg, the self-proclaimed spiritual advisor of the friends, interrupted. With a rising voice, and a deep crinkle in the center of her bushy brows, she proclaimed, "I prayed about this man of yours, and I feel led to tell you that he is a demon!" In concert, with eyes rolling, hair swinging, gold bracelets jingling, and giggles of aggravated appreciation, they said, "OK, Reg, we know. *All men are demons!*" This is the only point about Arrington on which they all agreed; indeed, he may have been trifling, but he was not a demon.

Even Patsy, the most tolerant and soft-spoken of this sorority, had had her fill of this so-called relationship. So when she spoke up this time, Sharlese listened with great attention. "Shar, you know I love you; we all love you. Just let me ask you one question without sounding too intrusive. "How much money have you loaned him to date? I remember all the times he has been in-between jobs. Then his mother needed medication after her surgery, and his car needed major repairs so that he could look for a job. He also had to have that new designer suit for the job interview. In other words, "How much are you in for?"

You, hey you, reading this book. I want to ask you the same thing, "How much are you in for?" Not just financially, but spiritually, emotionally, physically? Are you being paid back? If not now, when? You are not to be selfless with your purpose and destiny. Once you have realized that you are pouring your love into a reservoir that will not love you back, close the spout, baby!

Jesus has words to say about any type of "gaping hole" scenario:

And do not throw your pearls before hogs, lest they trample upon them with their feet and turn and tear you in pieces. (Matthew 7:6 AMP)

We all know that pearls are beautiful and valuable. What we must remember is that pearls are made deep within the center of the oyster while living in the wide expanse of the ocean. The formation of a pearl is a long and very slow process. The smaller pearls can take five to seven years to form, and the larger, more expensive ones can take up to twenty years. During the development of this treasured stone, the oyster encounters all types of fish in the ocean, yet it continues its process of cultivating something special within until the one who *recognizes* the value of the pearl takes the time to carefully attend to the oyster while plucking the pearl from its shell. Let me break it down for you: "Don't trade your bling for a bacon sandwich."

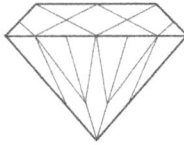

Pink Diamond

You have too much value to give yourself away to worthlessness!

SIGNS AND SYMPTOMS

Spiritually

He has no committed relationship with the Lord Jesus Christ. He resents godly attributes.

He shows no respect for chastity.

Emotionally

He makes little to no effort to provide you with any emotional support.

He does not give you compliments.

Often he may be cruel and even leans toward abusive.

He is negligent of how his actions and words negatively impact you.

CHAPTER 4

The Cracked-Pot Man

It's not what you think—not exactly, anyway. The *cracked-pot* guy is the most
elusive broken type of all. Yet I believe it is
the most commonly experienced of all frac-
tured relationships. It is like a car tire with
a small, undetected, pin-sized hole. The en-
try point and time of puncture will never
be known, but a steady and sure release of
air seeps from the tire. Initially, the tire
seemingly functions as though there are no
breaks or tears in its integrity. No doubt,
though, the tire is no longer performing at

its optimum capacity. It still rotates upon command, but it is now strained. Each time the tire is summoned to perform by the driver, more damage is done to the unattended rupture. Slowly the car leans into an unintended direction until the laceration is noticed. Usually, much damage has been caused by then. In the worst-case scenario, the little hole has the ability to morph into a fatal outcome.

"Daddy, even as a little girl, I enjoyed our car rides into the city, especially when it is just you and me." Simone settled into the car, automatically buckling her seat belt as she took in the familiar childhood scent. Her father was a great man, but stubborn in many ways. Even after several newly introduced fragrances and much persuasion, he still wore the same cologne that he had used for decades. The faint traces of his scent gently reminded her of the security of a loving family and joy-filled memories. "Yeah, Suga' Bear. We have spent countless hours burning rubber on this road. Some would say that this drive would be a drawback to living in the country and having to drive seventy miles into town for supplies. However, I relish it because it has always been the perfect space and time for me to spend with God and my family... especially my Suga' Bear." He flashed those kind eyes at Simone in the way that only a loving father could do, providing a glance that spoke without words of pride and joy.

As the reliable car moderately cruised around well-known curves, the scenery invoked the dreams of her tender youth. She recalled gazing at the dancing oak trees, wondering effortlessly about the world on the other side of them. The current interlude of silence in the car was welcomed as it allowed for the feelings she longed to experience again to glide over her soul. Each mile was reminiscent of her former self, her true self. The trusting intonation of her father's voice was a cordial intrusion to her walk down memory lane.

"Suga,' I often tell your mother how I felt the very first time I laid eyes on you. You were, and still are, the most beautiful creature I had ever seen since meeting your mother. I was a little scared to hold you at first because you were so tiny and fragile; I didn't want to break you. It took courage to take you in my arms and not drop you. That day I vowed to always take you in my arms and not drop you until the day that I die. I have watched you grow from a little, inquisitive girl up to a college-educated woman. That was another proud day of my life, watching my Suga' Bear walk across the stage and get a degree." He was not a man that many had witnessed crying, but today was different. As he spoke, the words began to crack against the air like the sound of a baseball and bat colliding in the heat of summer. "Aww, Daddy, that's so sweet." Simone smiled sheepishly.

"That is why...that is why I...I must get something off my chest. It has been tearing me to pieces." It was then that Simone noticed for the first time that her once virile father was aging. As he spoke, the wrinkles that were formerly just-noticeable lines began to fold in despair. "I know you are a grown woman now, but ever since you got with "what's-his-face" I don't recognize who you are anymore."

Startled that he would broach the subject, she became more attentive to his words. "As a matter of fact, everything has changed about you. You were always so independent; now you can't or won't make a decision without consulting this guy. You have always been surrounded by loving family and friends; since he's been in the picture, we rarely hear from you. Your work ethic has been marred to the point you can no longer maintain a job, let alone a career."

Simone knew that her father spoke the truth, and suddenly this truth became clearer than the brightness of the warm sun that flooded the car; she too began to weep silently. "My beautiful, vivacious daughter with the laughter that children dance to has become withdrawn, depleted, and obviously depressed. Look at you, you have lost your sense of style, your way, your everything... doggone...you have lost *you!*"

Overwhelmed by the weight of her mixed emotions of shame and anger, her slumped shoulders quaked. She was not mad at her father; no, she was mad at herself. How could she have lost herself? She felt ashamed that her father would live to see a day with her in this mess.

"Baby girl, your mother and I want only the best for you." The supply store was only a few more miles away. Simone was so wretchedly miserable at that moment, she wished that somehow she could become invisible and be transported to walk in the beautiful fields of daffodils just beyond the window. As he continued driving toward town, she saw the occasional cow and considered how oblivious the cows must be to heartache; all they had to do was graze and sleep.

"When I met your mother and fell in love with her, I promised God that if she said yes to marrying me, I would work every day to make her happy. I can stand before Him in the Judgment and know that I have done my level best to fulfill my promise these last forty-seven years. Our marriage is not perfect—no marriage is— but we are perfect for each other.

Suga' Bear, I want to see you with a man who recognizes you for the gift you are and vows to daily appreciate God for you." The silence that blanketed the car was not welcomed but necessary. The next few moments, days, and weeks would be a time of introspection for Simone. She would have to decide to either just exist with "what's-his-face" or get about the business of living.

The *cracked-pot* man mimics the tire analogy in that the integrity of your essence is punctured every time he puts a demand on you that alters the purpose that God has intended. It begins with small suggestions. When he notes your complicity, he perceives it as an invitation to ask for more, and he does. Little by little, as the days of life go by, he requires more from you to inflate himself. In his mind, it is impossible for both you and him to be full and fruitful. Your true self must deflate in order for him to survive.

The relationship does have some good things about it so that you overlook the signs that you are leaning in the opposite direction from where you first started. Time is this guy's greatest ally. He uses it like a skilled marksman calculating the precise moment to aim and release. In between the times of sipping the very life force from you, he gently numbs you with moments of joyful surprise. You read "hope" in his unannounced but desperately desired kind gestures. You think, perhaps, he is changing. Things are finally turning around for the better. This false sense of utopia is short-lived. It isn't until you hit the next pothole in the road of life that you realize you are no longer the person you used to be. Somewhere along this journey, you have altered the values that make you real to your true self. You no longer experience the emotional fitness that your soul supported in the past. How did you get here? How did *you* lose yourself?

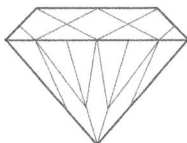

Pink Diamond

"Half a loaf of a man is better than no loaf of a man at all" is the second-biggest lie every told! Eve heard the biggest one.

Constant concession is ultimate suffocation. Everyone knows in order to maintain a productive and healthy relationship that "give and take" is mandatory. Both parties must give up selfish desires and self-centered motives. Sweetness, let me ask you something, "How much have you given and how much has he taken?"

It is time to do some tire kicking! Whip out that pressure gauge before you are sitting on the side of the road completely deflated and unable to move altogether. Examine who you were when you came into the relationship. Then compare her to who you are now. Is there a balance or do you need to align certain behaviors, words, or attitudes to bring things in sync with where you are supposed to be going? You may have to rotate some things by reprioritizing your time and efforts. Even if it means leaving the tires, the car, or the city, if he is abusive, *get out*! I'm just saying, plug the leak or get a new tire.

SIGNS AND SYMPTOMS

Your self-esteem has significantly declined. You have become isolated and depressed.

He manages every moment of your existence.

You are banned from healthy family and friendly relationships. When you consider being with him the rest of your life, death seems like a viable option.

He is verbally, emotionally, spiritually, and/or physically abusive.

CHAPTER 5

Paper or Plastic, Ma'am?

Lynne Lane Park is the idyllic country scene balancing nature's beauty and serenity. Its long natural trails through densely wooded areas provide the sublime cover for couples seeking a private refuge. The east side of this local lover's lane is home to a small but popular artificial lake. On any given weekend you will find a community of undemanding pleasure-seekers gathered around this provincial watering hole. Families with small children don safety vests as they gleefully paddle brightly colored plastic boats. Old men, whose faces and "big-fish" stories have weathered time, cast lines and converse reminiscently of days gone by, their memories only as faithful as the emotions that served them.

Occasionally, the chatter of old friends casually walking the expanse of the greens is mingled with the sounds of music playing in the ear of the avid jogger as she passes by, sprinting to desperately overcome the stress of a busied life. This flash of paradise is the perfect backdrop for the proclamation of love and commitment. These moments of happiness are but a foretaste for a lifelong joy of two people sharing their lives as one.

Madison and Josef chose to bring breadcrumbs to feed the geese this go round. It was their second time meeting at the park, but their fifth date. She found this man to be just as mysterious as the dusk that was settling on this fourth Saturday evening in May. They met online, and he wasted no time in asking her out. She was encouraged that he found her so interesting, and he moved quickly to begin to know her. Josef was easy to talk to. Before Madison realized it, hours would pass, and she had shared secrets of her past that not even some of her closest friends knew. Heck, she even discussed the breakdown of her previous relationships, and he understood perfectly. It was almost as though their hearts beat in sync, at first.

He was liberal with his compliments and so willing to overlook her apparent flaws and shortcomings. Perhaps she found him intriguing because of his job that required weekly travel, or the experiences he said he had as a highly restricted operation's agent for the government. She did research on the Internet to do a background check on him. When she could find no evidence supporting his adventures, he explained to her that all of the heroic exploits he had done were "classified." They were not available for public record because of the sensitive nature involved. Anyway, today was a time with a real live man sitting on the bench, not a virtual relationship sustained by typed characters in a small box on the computer screen.

"Boo, I am so glad that you were able to get away for a few hours to spend with me." Madison's voice was soft and gentle as she snuggled closer to him. Josef, with the pose of a masterful puppeteer, leaned into her, briskly rubbing against her full hips. "Baby, you know I try to spend as much time as I can with you." Gingerly using this as a segue, she responded, "I admit, I was a little concerned when I left all those messages for you by email and text, and it was days before you reached out to me." Josef then reached for her hands, methodically entwining his rough fingers through hers. "I know, I know, but we have talked about this over and over. In addition to my hectic work schedule, I am trying to keep my sanity in this crazy divorce thing. Man, she is using my kids against me!"

Madison, frustrated with the answer but not wanting to drive him away, rubbed his back. "I understand that women use their kids as pawns to tie men down, but tell me again, why are you still living in the same house with her? I can't stand the fact that I can't see you or call you when I want." Josef quickly stiffened and rapidly replied, "I am only there for my kids. I am committed to them. Please don't make me choose between you and them. I don't have feelings for her except that she is the mother of my three kids. If I leave her now, she will take all that I have. Can you please be the soft place for me to lay my head? She doesn't understand me like you do. Please, baby, please work with me on this." Madison slightly shifted her weight, sighing inwardly knowing that she was seeing Josef only so that she wouldn't have to go through the summer alone. "OK, hun." She relinquishes herself to yet another relationship that fills time and space. Madison and Josef both knew that this relationship was a temporary fling. He was never leaving his wife because that is where he wanted to be. Madison would never have Josef because he belonged to another. The sunset over the lake was beautiful that evening.

All successful businesses understand a very important investment principle: controlling the flow of resources. The idea is to spend the least amount of money, time, and labor to gain the highest possible return. Profit is the bottom line. Businesses know that sufficient funds must be allocated to marketing, location, staff, and production. Therefore they reduce their spending in areas that have the smallest impact on their bottom line. One area that businesses find in common to minimize their cost is the bags that will carry their products and goods home with the consumer. High-end boutiques and thrifts stores alike provide the same type of packaging at the close of a sale: paper or plastic bags. These bags are a staple in meeting a need in the huge world of retail. So miniscule is the monetary value, and thus quality, of these plastic and paper containers that they often must be doubled-bagged in order to be adequate. Few words can describe the frustration of carrying several bags of groceries from the car to the house in the cold and the rain, only to have the plastic bag split wide open en route. Eight raw eggs and their broken shells lay splattered in your driveway alongside the watery milk that is profusely flowing from its burst container. The bag was not durable enough to support the items that were placed into it. A waste of valuable resources and a mess are left behind.

The temporary nature of plastic and paper bags resembles a certain type of man in regards to a committed relationship. Let us call him "P&P" to shorten*paper-and-plastic* man for our discussion purposes. Upon a cursory examination of plastic and paper bags in retail, we can note several similarities with "P&P." The obvious is the fleeting integrity of each. However, the ability to endure the vicissitudes of life is essential. The very meaning of life is change! There are emotionally rainy days and cold days. You need someone who has the ability to not only support you, but who possesses

the capability to carry all the valuable resources that are yours: your visions,
dreams, hopes, and aspirations. The hard
days are the worst time for your resources
to be wasted. You need someone whose fiber of character is strong and resistant to
splitting or tearing under minimal stress. It
is necessary to have that "somebody" who
holds *you* while holding "it" together.

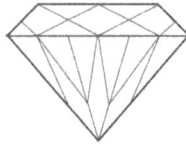

Pink Diamond

**He cannot support you if he
is not fully committed to you.**

You already know that you cannot expect a lot from Mr. "P&P," just like you
know that plastic and paper bags have limited functionality. When the clerk at the
store bags your products, you give no
thought of engaging in a lengthy and
meaningful relationship with the bags. You

clearly understand that they are a simple means to an end. They are not meant to be fashionable. You don't use them as accessories to your wardrobe. You give no attention to the label that is imprinted on the sides. All you want from the bag is to carry your belongings from point A to point B. Sadly, you can figure this out in the grocery store, but you often do not recognize it in your relationships.

In the beginning of the liaison, the man let you know that he was spiritually, emotionally, financially, and physically unavailable to you, and yet you daydreamed about him. You wrote your first name and his last name as you doodled and scribbled on paper. You co-signed with him for financial commitments. You divulged all of your personal information, social security number, ATM pin numbers, and passwords to your social media accounts. You may have even gotten pregnant with his baby, hoping to turn a temporary guy into a permanent man. Then, as his integrity buckled under the pressure, you became emotionally undone. Why—when you knew all the time?

The final observation about paper and plastic bags is the fact that they are cheap. They are so cost effective that they are given away to every customer who makes a purchase, without limits. You can even ask that your bags are doubled to secure your items, and the bagger does it without flinching because the bags have minor value to the bottom line. Paper and plastic bags are made by mass production, that is, the manufacturing of large amounts of products at a low cost per unit. Although quality does not have to be compromised in this process, it probably is for the paper and plastic bags that are distributed at the local market. You may be wondering, "How is a guy mass produced?" Certainly not on an assembly line! But his culture, mentality, and spirituality are all contributions to his overall make-up, as with everyone. You can prayerfully observe the people and things in his life that influence him and often determine the quality of person he is. Our society is shaped by an inundation of irreverence for God, disrespect of humanity, and the promotion of self-centeredness. Unfortunately, many of our men are responding to these concepts through the negative images, words, and actions produced by media sources. Regrettably, these profane attitudes and behaviors bleed into interpersonal relationships. Chivalry is not dead, but it is on life support.

There are so many temporary-minded men to choose from. They come in droves. They are online and in workplaces, churches, schools, prisons, and everywhere. They wear jeans, custom suits, clerical garb, and uniforms. They have many titles and occupations. Nonetheless, as soon as they are revealed for who they are, you have a choice. When asked, "Paper or plastic, ma'am," you should respond, "Neither! I deserve better."

SIGNS AND SYMPTOMS

He is vague about specific details of his personal life.

You have contact only in a virtual world or only by cell phone. He is constantly unavailable on holidays, weekends, and nights. You have never met any of his family or close friends.

You can't call him; he must call you.

He has a long history of very short relationships.

He wants you to give everything up front while he has minimal investment in time, information, and resources.

CHAPTER 6

The Untempered-Glass Man

The *untempered-glass* man has the *potential* to be a great guy. Remember the word "potential" because later we will have a caveat about it. He has all the elements that are required to contain your love without significant gaps, holes, or tears. He has the potential to match your capacity of giving love and receiving love. So, you ask, "What is the problem?" The *untempered-glass* man is unrestrained or lacks self-control. Often this is due to a lack of maturity. He simply has not grown up! His body is certainly developed — and nicely developed at that. He can hold down a job. He can engage in intelligent conversation and friendly banter. He may even be a father. But! (That critical three-letter word "but" carries a ton of weight.) He is emotionally immature. We could write a library of books discussing all the reasons that he is immature, but at the close of the day the reasons do not matter. It is what it is. However, the good thing about this guy is, not all hope is lost.

"Jones, please pick up the phone. I have left countless messages for you over the last three days, and you refuse to return my calls...Jones...Jones!...Jones!" Kelly sighs with tremendous vexation as she ends the call, throwing her expensive smartphone on the bed. Her flushed face and puffy eyes have paid the toll of this "on again-off again" relationship with her boyfriend of two years. The "ignore you because I am mad at you game" is a staple cycle in this tumultuous courtship. "Uuugh, I could understand if he were mad at something that made sense, but these stupid little, simple little...uuugh!" Kelly growls while stomping to the kitchen to dip her third bowl of cookie dough ice cream. As she tranquilizes her nerves with shots of sugary desserts, she flops across her couch wondering how this really cool guy could have such torrid tantrums.

Excitement ran high and competition even higher as the judges of the annual artist's exhibit tallied their votes. The blue ribbon prize served as an incentive for many talented people to showcase their work. The winner would receive a significant monetary prize, an interview in the local newspaper, and mention in the upcoming mayoral address. Kelly's friends giggled in hopeful support of the oil portrait she had submitted. It was rumored to be a sure winner. Another crowd favorite was the elaborate hand sculpture created by Jones, the son of the town's most prominent attorney. Jones was known not only for his unique artistic ability, but also as quite the lady's man. Those who had fallen prey to his charm told of beautiful walks on the beach at sunset, romantic dinners, exquisite gifts, and passionate, gentle kisses. The challenge was that he would commit to no one. He was as much a mystery man as he was a good catch.

The crowd came to a frenzy as Mr. Jabbo walked staunchly across the platform. He grabbed the microphone and, after clearing his throat, proceeded to announce the third-place winner. The applause was amicable but guarded in anticipation of the next two winners. "The second-place prize goes to Jones Bismark." The assembly erupted into thunderous applause because if Jones won second place, Kelly would be a shoo-in for first place. Annoyed by the uncontained outburst of the onlookers, Mr. Jabbo raised his voice when announcing, "The first-place, blue-ribbon winner for the annual artist exhibit this year is...Kelly Stewart!" The exhilaration of winning was so overwhelming that Kelly turned and grabbed the first person she could reach and planted a big, fat, wet kiss on his mouth. All of a sudden, a tingling feeling rushed down her body, more satisfying and confusing than the winning moment could award her. Every fiber of her being was penetrated by this sensation. She was flooded with an intense awareness that her soul mate was the recipient of her unbridled reaction. Kelly and Jones both jumped back startled because each recognized when staring into the other's eyes that something spiritual had happened. Kelly not only won first place at the exhibit that day, but she also won Jones's heart.

Their journey over the past several months has been riddled with plentiful arguments, heated hysterics, and just plain ole' drama. Jones seemed to always major in the minors and minor in the majors. Concerning things that were seemingly of great importance to the progression or even stability of the relationship, Jones was cavalier. Sometimes he was downright thoughtless and rude. When Kelly wanted to sit and talk about opportunities for improvement, Jones would grow silent or, worse, he would began to hum the most dreadful sounding song imaginable. He refused to handle the adult-level issues. As long as things were fun and lighthearted, and he did not need to show accountability, Jones was perfect. The moment that Jones needed to stand up and be responsible, he baulked at whomever or whatever dispensed the guidelines to him. Ultimately, he would distance himself from the relationship. He would not respond to text messages or voice mails and had, on occasion, blocked Kelly from all of his social media accounts. As he did every time, after a few days he would slowly come around, never admitting or apologizing for his childish behavior.

This time was different. Kelly was just fed up with the same old, same old all the time. As she finished the last spoon of ice cream, it was in some strange way symbolic of the end of what could have been the perfect relationship. She must come to terms with the truth in front of her. There were torrents of passion for the same interest but minimal progression to a well-rounded mutual respect. What was kind of cute at first had become the signs of an underdeveloped interpersonal skill set. Jones was a bona fide untempered glass man. Should she wait until he matured or cut her losses?

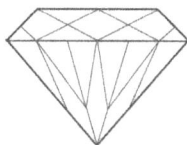

Pink Diamond

**Great charisma does not
equate to good character!**

The purpose of tempering glass is to increase its ability to be flexible and strong, and to manage how it breaks. Tempered glass is used in car windows, public buildings, and furniture. It is approved for its safety. Glass is not naturally tempered. It requires a specific technique to promote its ability to safeguard. The tempering system is a science that involves the glass being taken through a series of processes. Upon completion, the glass is highly recommended to provide the best protection against breakage. There is a compelling parallel to untempered glass and the untempered man. With both, the process by which tempering occurs is arduous and long, but it yields a highly desirable vessel.

The method used to change the character of the untempered glass is called *annealing*. This procedure employs the use of extremity and time. In glass, annealing prevents internal stress by the involvement of high heat and a slow cooldown. Note that heat, time, and cold all must work in concert to produce the desired product. The same is true in character building for the untempered man. It is a combination of things that work together to teach him restraint and self-control. In his life, he must endure some ups and downs. Through the process of time, he should learn temperance.

During the annealing process, the longer the heating cycle, the more stress is removed from the glass. The slower the cool down, the less chance the glass has of becoming stressed again. It is important to allow a man the time to grow, mature, and develop spiritually, emotionally, and physically. If you commit to him when he is untempered in any or all of these areas, you will commit to sharing with him in his annealing process. You will join him as he endures his extremes. Please note there are no guarantees of the time it could take or that he will complete the process at all. You may be in it for a long ride going nowhere or possibly, after a very long while, you will have the reward of a vessel of honor.

Remember the word, "potential"? The meaning of the word is a combination of two opposites; possible as opposed to actual. The capacity is certainly present, but there are no guarantees. As a nurturer (see chapter 1) you see that a guy may have the capacity to be all that you think you need and want. So you begin the task of trying to transfer potential energy, that which is stored up deep inside him, and make it kinetic energy, something that should move itself. Sister, as long as you are doing it for him, he will never benefit from being tempered. It is his process, not yours! His experience with God, humanity, and life will transform a guy who has just "potential" into a man who is actually working toward a satisfying relationship with you.

The need for strength and flexibility in a companion does not necessitate explanation. However, the management of the breaking points is vitally important to discern. One of the key advantages to tempering glass is that it can endure a lot of pressure before it comes to a breaking point. A man similar in character is the one with whom you want to travel the road of life, someone who will handle an abundance of weight. Life offers many obstacles, afflictions, and troubles. You do not want someone who cannot control his impulses and cravings. However, you should desire someone who has endured the test of time and withstood it.

Realistically, there are times in every person's life when a breaking point will be experienced. After carrying a load for a long time, a person may feel overwhelmed and buckle. How this person breaks could be detrimental to you. Tempered glass, if it is ever broken, does not shatter into sharp pieces. Instead, because of its process, it will usually stay within the window frame. If it falls to the ground, it will fragment into small round beads so that its ability to injure is minimized. A tempered man will do the same. Because of his process, if he buckles under the load, he will at least stay in the framework of your relationship. If he falls, he will make sure that he minimizes your exposure to what he is going through so that your damage, if any, is minimal.

Should Kelly continue her relationship with Jones? Should she put the relationship on hold and give him a chance to mature while taking the chance that they might not reunite? What about you? What should you do? It all depends on what you are willing to go through with him *if* he *ever* grows up. Are you willing to deal with tantrums and pouting for an unknown amount of time? Are you willing to not hold a place of high priority in his life? Are you willing to risk your well-being while he is "sowing his wild oats"? Perhaps your guy has the mentality of a college male living in a frat house. Or maybe he is the poster child for a "mama's boy." Whatever the developmental delay is or its reason, you must identify him as an *untempered glass* man and you must make your decision to stay or leave.

SIGNS AND SYMPTOMS

He is impatient.

He lacks consideration.

He is short-tempered.

He is selfish.

He is flirtatious with other women.

He lacks commitment.

He is unreliable.

He is crude and childish and is a game player.

CHAPTER 7

Flesh and *Boner*

Please pardon my colloquialism or slang, if you will, in using the term "boner." But I needed to get your attention! The preceding chapters discussed the brokenness of certain types of men. This chapter will examine why you continue to pour your love into these broken vessels. Intimate relationships are uniquely different from familial ones. You are born or adopted into a family. Initially, you have no choice about those relationships. However, you choose your friends and mates. If you continue to choose the same "man" in a different body type, hair color, age, or status at different stages of your life, dear heart, the problem is not so much the man, the problem is *you*! This chapter will expose common reasons as to why you are wasting your time, your love, and your life.

The primary reason that women continue to pour their love into broken vessels, even after they have become aware of the defect, is that they themselves are fragmented. Let me be very clear. There is no perfect man or woman, save Jesus Christ alone! However, there are people who are whole. What is the difference? A perfect person is without sin or flaw. A whole person finds completeness in his or her relationship with Christ Jesus. Spiritually, emotionally, and socially that person is intact. As members of humanity, everyone experiences bruising and dents as we bump into each other in life, particularly as we engage in interpersonal relationships. How we recover from those incidents and accidents determines our wholeness.

The deepest level of brokenness is experienced in the area of spirituality. If there is a break in a person's relationship with God, it will chip away at every other part of the person. It is impossible to have whole, satisfactory, and happy relationships with humans if you are not in right fellowship with God. (John 3:7, Romans 10:8–10).

The second area where some women are damaged is in the soul. The soul consists of the mind and the emotions. It is the place where inclinations, cravings, and decisions are made. If this region has been injured but not healed, the woman is broken. It is a known fact that hurting people will hurt people. When you chose someone to be in your life to heal your heart, you are extending an invitation to utter devastation. It is an unfair burden for someone else to be responsible for healing the hurts of your past. Whether the trauma occurred in your childhood, adolescence, or adulthood, it is *your* responsibility to get the healing you need. You owe it to yourself to be emotionally strong. A healthy person wants to partner with another healthy person to enjoy life. Few healthy people seek out and commit their lives to spiritually and/or emotionally sick people.

Another reason women turn over their precious emotions to unworthy men is that they choose to settle. There is little to no discretion in the standard of man that they will accept. (Chapter 9 will give you specifics on how to manage this portion of relationships.) There is an old-fashioned saying I love: "Just because he is wearing britches don't make him a man." Some women have bought into the hype that all the good men are taken. That's a lie! Other women have low or no self-esteem, which we have already touched on. If there are no worthy companions in your circle, be by yourself until *you* expand the parameter of your circle. (See chapter 9 for further discussion of this subject). In the meantime, don't waste your greatest asset: *you*!

Another thing to which some daughters of Zion fall prey is that they are looking for the wrong things. Most people want someone who is good looking. True enough that there should be some physical attraction. However, do not allow that to navigate the direction of your ship because there are some good-looking devils out there! Look for good strong character. Observe how he treats you and others with whom he is in a relationship. What is their level of faithfulness to their current commitment? Hear beyond what they say to the words that they are not saying. Do you leave their presence whole or broken? These are just a few of the things you should begin to look for in a man.

This final paragraph of the chapter will be devoted to the *foolish* women: You who stay with Mr. Broken Bozo because you are too trifling to be in a relationship with Brother Boaz. You know the man is married. But you think you have accomplished something because he belongs to someone else. The true standard of a real woman is that she can get her own man and not have to take someone else's in the process. Also, to the woman who feels that she has to

have sex in order to get and keep a man: if sex is the only thing you have to keep him, you are going to end up alone anyway, because most women have a vagina. Yep, it is pretty common among women. Finally, to the woman who enters into a relationship with a good man to destroy him, take his best assets, and use him: please feel welcome to taken the broken men who refused to get healed because you belong together.

CHAPTER 8

The Honorable Vessel

*But in a great house there are not only
vessels of gold and silver, but also of wood
and clay, some for honor and some for dis-
honor. Therefore if anyone cleanses himself from the latter, he will be a vessel for
honor, sanctified and useful for the Mas-
ter, prepared for every good work.*

(2 Timothy 2:20–21)

There is a huge amount of single, available,
straight, honorable men in the world today!
The world's population is over seven billion people. You have to know that all men

are not dogs. All men are not evil and dirty. There is a group of men who are honorable vessels. They are honest and fair. They have integrity and are respectable. They are courteous, and some are even chivalrous! Just this morning, many of them prayed to God for a good wife. In order to understand the truth of these vessels, we must go back to our Maker.

God has a tendency to deal with the image of vessels. He indubitably places a high premium on how something is contained. This can be seen beginning with His Creation to the fulfillment of His Redemptive Plan. Genesis describes in detail how God formed Adam with His own hand from the dust of the ground. That hull of flesh lay lifeless upon the earth until God breathed in it His Breathe "and man became a living soul" (Genesis 2:7). Humanity, God's most prized creation, was made a vessel to contain His Breathe.

A person is comprised of three components. He or she is a spirit who possesses a soul and lives in a body. The soul of a person, the emotions and intellect, does not wander about the universe without the ability to experience the tangible world. That is done through the vessel called "the body." Within the soul, God created an innate desire for humanity to be relational. We long for meaningful and satisfying relationships with other people. For many, aesthetical virtues draw the attention of a prospective mate. Our society highly esteems the external beauty of the body. Ultimately, however, it should be the essence of the soul that drives the decision to enter into a committed relationship.

Sin methodically ravished the soul of humans leaving behind a carnage of emotional vessels, fragmented in varying degrees. God's answer to this problem was enclosed in a vessel, **Jesus**, who is God incarnate. God wrapped Himself in a vessel of flesh to dwell among us. His vessel became broken so that we could be made whole. Although Jesus' work at Calvary was completed, we have a progressive consecration to God that we live daily and with the people we choose to love. There are no flawless people, but there is a perfect partner for you.

So far we have addressed vessels that are broken. They all have the opportunity to be repaired and made into vessels of honor through Jesus Christ. In addition, there are vessels who are whole and are waiting to be united with another vessel of honor. So let's take a close look at the characteristics of an honorable vessel.

When you want to optimize the benefits of all the great features of your newest electronic device, you consult the manufacturer's manual. The same is true with an honored vessel. It is imperative to consult the Bible, God's manufacturer's manual for humanity, to maximize our relationships. I love the Bible's honesty because it shows us the best and the worst of people. It is a book that illustrates humanity's triumphs and failures. There are many people in the Word of God who qualify for "Honored Vessel of the Year." We will consider only four gentlemen for our archetypes.

LOVE

The deepest yearning of every woman is to be loved unconditionally; the love that looks beyond physical flaws and human frailties, the kind of love that allows you to be you without apology, explanation, or shame. Real love. Felt love. Sensual love. Love that has the ability to transform secret dreams into public realities. Sacrificial love such that he will die in your place if necessary. The type of love that you imagine only Jesus himself could give. Jesus? Yes, Jesus! He is the standard by which the Bible commands a man to love his wife. This concept is found in Ephesians 5:25-28.

Isaac is the "Man of the Hour" when it comes to loving his woman. Isaac and Rebekah's entire love story can be found in the twenty-fourth chapter of Genesis. There are some key points I want to highlight about their initial encounter. The entire love hook-up was a divine intervention. It was a season of transition for Isaac's father, and he wanted to see his son fulfilled in a godly marriage before he died. He sent his servant to a specific place looking for a specific type of woman. Needless to say, she would be classified as an "honored vessel." The servant arrived at the appointed place and waited for the appointed time. In his prayer, he asked God that the right woman would carry a *pitcher,* or vessel, that would contain the water needed to quench his thirst and that of his camel. Later that day Rebekah went to the well with a pitcher on her shoulder. The servant recognized that her vessel had the capacity to bless someone else for she used her vessel in kindness and thoughtful consideration. Her vessel *identified* her for favor. But, what *qualified* her for her great blessing was that her water pitcher was whole and so was she. The Bible describes her as beautiful and chaste. After proper communication with her family and their consent, she broadened her horizon. Her husband was not in that place. Supported by the godly counsel of her parents, she enlarged the parameters of her circle.

As Isaac was in the field mediating, he looked up to see coming toward him the camel that Rebekah was riding. When Rebekah saw Isaac, she immediately jumped off her camel. (That's what I call "an eyeful"). The first words out of her mouth were, "Who is this man?" The servant informed Isaac about all that had happened, and proper introductions were made. Isaac took her to his recently deceased mother's tent. He did not co-habit with her. He made her his wife, not "wife-like." The Bible says, "And he loved her." Because he "manned up," married her, and loved her, he received comfort from her for the grief he suffered from his mother's death.

So let me draw the dotted lines of this Biblical love story to our contemporary society:

1. God will divinely intervene in your relationships if you seek Him.

2. There is an appointed season when things are set in motion toward your committed relationship. Often, it is

behind the scenes, and you are not aware that it is happening.

3. A good man already has a specific type of woman in mind that he wants or needs.

4. There is an appointed time within your appointed season.

5. There is a specific place where the initial encounter will transpire.

6. You must be found handling your business. Rebekah would have missed it if she were lazy.

7. You must be kind and generous of spirit (not your bank account). She received gifts before she gave gifts.

8. You must be whole yourself.

9. You must handle things that are whole. Do not involve yourself in questionable and shady activities.

10. Depend heavily on godly counsel. Submit yourself to people who can recognize the purpose of God in your life.

11. In your decision-making, involve loving family and friends who have your best interest at heart.

12. Be willing to enlarge the parameters of your circle. Take a class, volunteer at a charitable event, or begin to travel.

13. Open your eyes and *recognize* when you see a good man.

14. Do not miss your blessing because he is working in a field instead of wearing a custom suit and silk tie. Thank God he is working!

15. No Ringy…No Thingy!

16. When a man gives you his love, you comfort his heart and you make his life comfortable.

Provision

Boaz' picture should be next to the word "provider" in the dictionary. He defines what it means for a man to make provision for his woman. Ruth was the object of Boaz' love and affection; their love story is found in the Book of Ruth. Before they met, though, Ruth was married and widowed at an early age. Because of her extraordinarily loving relationship with her mother-in-law Naomi, Ruth decided to abandon her pagan religion, move from her home country, and follow Naomi to her homeland. They eventually came to a place where Ruth gleaned in the field, which is the gathering of leftover crops. One day Boaz, the owner of said field, saw her at work and inquired about her. The field hands were able to report that Ruth was a good worker. Boaz then told her not to go into any other field but his and to stay with the women within his field. He commanded the other men not to touch her, and when she was thirsty, the young men had to give her water they had drawn. When she asked why he was so fa-

vorable toward her, he told her that it was
due to her exceptional kindness to her
mother-in-law. Afterward, he provided a
meal for her. He then gave orders for the
men to leave her extra grain that was easy
for her to gather.

Ruth shared with Naomi what had tran-
spired. Naomi rejoiced and informed Ruth
that Boaz was a distant relative of hers. Ac-
cording to Jewish law at the time, he could
marry Ruth after a process of certain
events. Naomi educated Ruth on how to
conduct herself in a manner such that Boaz
would find her attractive and ready for
marriage. Ruth faithfully followed Naomi's
wise counsel. Eventually, Boaz was so
moved by the inner beauty, fortitude, and
humility of this young woman that he went
to the governing council to ask for permis-
sion to marry Ruth. They, of course, con-
sented. Boaz and Ruth lived happily ever
after. Their destiny included Jesus in their
family lineage generations later. God has a
divine plan.

The book of Ruth encapsulates several important lessons in securing a committed relationship with an honorable man:

1. You can begin again! Ruth's husband died at an early age, but her heart was not closed to love again.

2. You must have the capacity to love beyond normal expectations. It was Ruth's love and loyalty that led her on a path to a satisfying committed relationship.

3. You must leave your idols! Cast down anything or anyone that is sitting on the throne of your heart that is not the True and Living God!

4. You must abandon things in your culture, lifestyle, and ideologies that are contrary to the purpose of God in your life.

5. You should be willing to explore various options. For Ruth, it was relocat-

ing under the supervision of her spiritual parent, Naomi.

6. You must be industrious. Work hard so you earn the right to rewards.

7. You must live a life that speaks a positive testimony about your good character.

8. You must speak up! Be prepared to present yourself with clarity of mind and articulation of speech.

9. You must be humble enough to receive the instructions given for your benefit from the honorable man in your life and wise enough to follow them.

10. You must communicate openly and honestly about the progression of your budding relationship with trusted mentors.

11. You should obey wise counsel when you receive it.

12. You must prepare yourself to go the extra mile to engage an honorable man. The payoff is worth your efforts.

13. You should calm down and wait until all the proper channels of authority have been appropriately handled before making a permanent commitment. If it is right, it can wait until it is done the right way.

14. You can have an enduring love and legacy.

Safety

The Department of Defense could learn certain security strategies from Joseph, Jesus' stepfather. Joseph and Mary are often relegated to the Christmas Holiday season only. However, Joseph epitomizes the man of honor who protects his family. Safety is thought to be near the base of humanity's hierarchal needs. God places a high premium on the issue of safety in regards to

those belonging to Him. Jesus, the only be-
gotten Son of God, made a journey into this
earthly realm through the womb of His
mother Mary. He experienced the stages of
infancy, early childhood, adolescence, and
adulthood. God would choose only a man
whom He trusted to protect and guard His
greatest asset, *His* Son. He determined to
choose a man who would appropriately
love His son and not molest him. He select-
ed a man who was a strong male role model. A man whom Jesus saw loving and pro-
tecting His mother and her child. God
tagged a man who had the ability to safeguard his family's lives and, more im-
portantly, shield their destinies. Joseph was
hand picked by God to be Jesus' stepfather.
What an auspicious honor!

The first mention of Joseph has to do
with his family heritage. He was of the lineage of Abraham. This fact is telling because it lets us know that Joseph was a man
who understood the power of connectivity.
He was not only connected to a people, but
also he was connected to the promise of a

coming savior. His upbringing embedded in him that God's plan for Israel would be significant in his own future.

Joseph was a man of commitment. When he splashed on the pages of the Bible, he was engaged to Mary. As a man of God, he would respect Mary's purity and chastity as a virgin. They were engaged and she still remained a virgin. Initially, when Joseph found out that Mary was pregnant, but he was not the father, he could have reacted violently and vindictively. Instead, the depth of his character prevented him from making a public disgrace of her. Rather, he decided to handle things secretly. Even when Mary's behavior looked doubtful, his character required him to protect her reputation.

Joseph had the ability to dream and receive instructions through them. The Scripture tells us of three significant dreams that subsequently protected his family and the plan of God. In the first dream, an angel delivered to him the Word of God regarding the plan for his life and his family's lives.

At this juncture, we learn three things about this honorable vessel. He had the ability to receive the Word of God, he was obedient to the Word he received, and he had the courage to be a witness to what had not ever happened before—immaculate conception! As soon as he awoke from the dream, he married Mary. The second and third dreams, although similar in purpose, reveal the depth of Joseph's spiritual aptitude. Each time he was told a specific place to take his family for safety and to their destiny. Each time he responded quickly to the divine instruction he received.

The Bible tells us that Joseph guarded the spirituality of his family. He was the only human eyewitness to the birth of Jesus. On two occasions we observe Joseph leading his family to participate in godly assemblies. The first is when he took Mary and Jesus into the temple for Jesus' dedication to God. The second scenario is twelve years later when the family made their pilgrimage to the temple to celebrate Passover. We later learn that Joseph was a "working man," a carpenter by trade. Joseph was a man of solid character who set the benchmark for how an honorable vessel protects the life, purpose, and destiny of his woman.

Joseph's life reads as a "How-to Book" in successful modernday relationships:

1. A man who can sustain healthy, long-term relationships has a greater understanding of the dynamics involved in commitment. If you are the *only* person in the whole wide world who understands him...*run!* You need to become the *former* woman in his life that *understood* him. Let's be real. There are seven billion people on the earth today, and no one else can figure him out but *you?* That has the potential to be problematic.

2. A man who has the restraint to honor God and you by not having any type of sexual relations will have a higher

probability of faithfulness to you in marriage.

3. A man who will safeguard your heart and defend your reputation is a "keeper."

4. A man who has the ability to make plans and put them into action is good. The man who puts legs to his dreams and does not just "talk the talk," is a man worth walking with.

5. A man who makes a promise and keeps it is good. Promises, promises, promises. After *all* this time, but he still has not married you yet? Humph!

6. A man you perceive to have been entrusted by God with a word, idea, or work may be someone you should consider trusting as well.

7. A man of honor who will take the lead in taking his family into the

Presence of God is an honorable vessel.

Considering the example of Joseph, when accepting dates, invitations, and opportunities from men, please post a prominent sign that says, "Working Men Only Need Apply." Also consider that safety is not only paramount in regards to protection from physical harm, it also encompasses the total *you*: your spirit, soul, body, hopes, secrets, children, and destiny.

CHAPTER 9

You Pay Dearly for Your Learning

In a few decades of life coaching and many more years of personal experience, I have learned various lessons in human nature. One thing for sure is that every relationship has its own code of conduct, communication, and understanding. It would be impossible to pen a document to describe each individual relationship in the world. However, I have acquired some practices that are full of wisdom for many scenarios.

1. Pray. Pray. Pray. A main subject in your prayer life should be any person you are thinking about weaving into the fabric of your life and destiny.

2. Create a list of characteristics for your "perfect man." Remember, there are no flawless people in the world, including you. There is, however, someone who is perfect *for you* in the sense of loving you correctly and complimenting your life's purpose. The best time to create this list is when you are not in a relationship so you have a clearer palette of thought, and you are not trying to factor in your current guy (I will give those of you who are currently in a relationship a different list to compose next).

A. Prayerfully and quietly, without distraction, begin to write down and enumerate the character traits that are absolutely essential for this guy to possess. These are the attributes that are nonnegotiable for any reason. No exceptions!

B. Then list the things about your "perfect guy" that you prefer, but about which you can be flexible. Good character is never an option. These things could be something like height, weight, and such. Itemize each detail based upon your criteria of priority. List what is most important to you down to "it would be good but it's really OK if they don't have this one."

C. Be specific. The more details the better. The longer the list the better.

D. Did I say pray? You may not complete this list in one sitting, but each time you revisit it, give it everything that you have. Too much is depending on the outcome to trivialize this task.

E. Keep the list in a safe place and review it from time to time. You might make adjustments as you grow and develop. You most certainly will adopt changes when exiting a bad relationship.

F. When you meet someone new, refer to your list. If he fails any of the nonnegotiable portion of your list. don't waste your life or time. Cut him loose before you are too emotionally invested.

G. Be patient...and pray.

H. If the guy passes the nonnegotiable part of the list, continue to move down to your "preferred seating section" and go from there.

I. Not every single item on your list may come with your perfect guy. But you should have all of your non-negotiables and a reasonable amount of your preferred. Of course, pray.

In a Broken-Vessel Relationship:

Create the same list as above and try not to think of your current guy, or that will sway what it is you really want. Second, write a separate outline that has a "Pro" and a "Con" side.

Honestly list all of the pros and all of the cons about your current relationship so that it's in black and white for you. Then take your pro-and-con list and measure it against your "perfect guy list." What do you really have?

1. Seek godly counsel. Do not keep your relationship or its issues a secret from trusted, wise counselors. They should be able to give you insight, advice, and criticism without

bias. Please do not receive wise counsel but disregard it because it is not what you want to hear. Prayerfully weigh and consider following their instructions.

2. Professional counseling/therapy is a great tool in determining your success in a relationship. If you are a broken vessel, seek help. If you are in a relationship with a broken vessel, seek help.

3. Trust the support of loving family and friends. It is a red flag if you feel you must hide him and keep the relationship a secret. Do not be so quick to defend him. Hurry to defend your destiny. A stand-up guy wants to meet the people in your life who are most important to you.

4. Time is your most valuable asset. Use it to your advantage.

5. Most of all make sure your relationship with God is right before you

engage in a committed relationship with a man.

6. These are some things that I have learned along the way that I want to pass on to you. May God make you whole and unite you with an honorable vessel so that your union may glorify God and fulfill both your purposes.

Pouring My Love in Broken Vessels
The Relationship Reference Guide

Are you tired of being emotionally and spiritually drained from giving your best in a relationship only to receive little to nothing in return?

Why do you keep choosing the "same man" in a different body?

Do you find yourself daydreaming, even fantasizing, about being in a better relationship with someone else?

The Ultimate thought-provoking Resource for Relationships!

> ➢ You will discover the core problem in your relationship.

> ➢ You will learn how to identify concealed character flaws in a potential partner that are relationship killers.

> ➤ You will recognize areas of broken-ness in your own life that allow you to be enticed into ill-fated relation-ships.

> ➤ You will become empowered to make good choices that will produce great relationships.

Each chapter provides a detailed **Sign and Symptoms List.**

Pouring My Love into Broken Vessels : The Relationship Reference Guide was written out of Kimberly Massery's deep reservoir of wisdom, sourced from twenty years of public service including seven years as a lead pastor. She delivers unique insight and guidance into the disciplines of a healthy and happy life. Step by step, she effectively coaches you how to avoid wasting your life, love, and destiny in dissatisfying and unfulfilled relationships.

ABOUT THE AUTHOR

Kimberly W. Massey is a senior pastor, life coach, executive leader, conference speaker, and TV and radio personality. Her message is informed, articulate, and relatable to all audiences. She is the proud mother of Gene and Abrae'.

www.kimberlymassey.com

Gebrae Publishing Group